witness to that light

PALMETTO
P U B L I S H I N G
Charleston, SC
www.PalmettoPublishing.com

Copyright © 2024 by John D. Shreve

All rights reserved

First Edition

Hardback ISBN: 979-8-8229-3339-2
Paperback ISBN: 979-8-8229-3340-8
eBook ISBN: 979-8-8229-3341-5

witness to that light

GETTING THE
GREEN LIGHT
FROM GOD
Continues...

JOHN D. SHREVE

TABLE OF CONTENTS

INTRODUCTION

First, let me explain the title of this book. It's an abbreviated version of Scripture: John 1:7. (See Chapter One.) Second, it's a continuation of my first book: Getting the Green Light from God. Read this book. Or, read that book. Read both books!

Chapter One explains the titles of both books. The other chapters are my own way of, I guess, preaching. I hope you will read both of my books, and most importantly, find them inspiring and helpful as you walk and find your path to Jesus and the Almighty.

A fair warning to readers: Topics of human sexuality and anatomy are mentioned in Chapter Three. Nothing crude or obscene, just in a matter-of-fact manner.

PREFACE

I am still a Sinner. Allow me to explain: God gave us Ten Commandments to follow. Jesus, two (when pressed). Of course, Jesus knew the hearts of those pressing Him, and, in typical Jesus-style, put these men of education and cloth back in their places with His Word. His words were and are Truth. One cannot successfully rebut "truth."

To love God with all my heart, mind, and soul, I have failed. To love my neighbor as Jesus loved us, I have also failed. So, the Truth cannot be changed with words, or my choice of them.

This being my second book, one can still notice my amateur writing skills, but again, the words about God and Jesus are the most important messages to convey. If you've read my first book, thanks! If you bought it, too, thank you! And if you bought this one as well, THANK YOU! When you're done reading and you've closed the back cover, I hope you're that much closer to the Almighty!

CHAPTER ONE

THRIFT STORE BIBLE

SO...I WROTE A BOOK! NOT just any book, not a self-help or fiction novel, I wrote a book about the Almighty, God! I've had thoughts of writing a book before, because I kind of think I have some genius to me, but never did I think I would write a book about a personal divine experience.

Getting the Green Light from God is the title. The year is 2020, I'm pretty sure. The date is December 26th, I'm sure. The time is about 1:30 a.m. I'm asleep in my bed at home in Austin, Texas. My eldest son Matthew sends me a text that says, "Merry Christmas." Being a light sleeper, I awake and read the text. I honestly can't remember if I became emotional or choked up some, seeing how I'd already thought I wasn't going to hear from any of my kids at Christmas. Regardless, I do recall saying aloud, "Thank you, God!" I didn't get out of bed, nor did I turn on a light. I just rolled over, opened my phone, maybe did a little boo-hooing, and spoke those 3 powerful words.

I got comfy again to go back to sleep, left-side laying, and just as I was starting to drift, a green light appears outside the bigger window of the bedroom. There are mini-blinds on the window and what I'm seeing is mini-blind images illuminated by green light, and it's getting greener. This window is to my right, or behind me since I'm on my left side. I am clueless as

3

to what is going on and I don't turn over or around to look that way. I'm fully awake now and my heart is beating like a drum. The green light remains at this window for about 15-20 seconds. Now, the light moves to the other bedroom window. It's a smaller window, also with mini-blinds, but this one has a curtain on it. I kept the curtain closed some with a clothespin and only the top area of the blinds is visible. It was in this top spot where the green light appeared, and it was as if the blinds disappeared so that the light could be seen.

And there, I witnessed a living green light, about the size of a basketball. There was movement within and on the edges. I witnessed the light for about 15 or 20 seconds. I had thoughts that my heart may just plop outside of my chest! Other than my heart pounding, I heard absolutely no noise. The light disappeared quickly, not a slow fade, just . . . gone. My heart rate did not normalize until at least 15 or 20 minutes had passed. Although my thoughts didn't know it at the time, my body, my flesh, my heart, knew what I had just witnessed and what was so close to it: the Creator of every cell and fiber of my being. I assumed my heart was sensing fear, but it wasn't. It was celebrating the presence of its Creator! My heart was saying, "Oh, my God," literally, "You are here!" In the Bible, there are many references to God "searching the hearts" of people. I can only conclude that God, heard my sincere thanks and saw something that we cannot see. And perhaps, since God saw something that impressed Him a little, He figured He would impress this John guy a little, but it would actually be a lot! Perhaps?

A few years before my green-light event, I bought a pre-owned Bible from a thrift store in Dripping Springs, Texas. They had several to pick from so I picked out the one in the best condition. It's a New International Version. I didn't have a Bible of my own, so I figured that I should have one. The backstory to this Bible is very important, as I will now explain.

My green-light book was complete by February, 2023, and I had already received my free copies of it from the publisher. Well, one evening in this February, I was watching a program on a Christian channel. The program had to do with the Book of John, and for some reason I found this Book very interesting, so I decided to open up my used Bible and check it out. Wow! Here it is: Chapter 1, verse 7 – "He came as a witness to testify concerning that light, so that through him all men might believe." On the last 2 letters of "light" -- the "h" and the "t" – there is a dark GREEN mark! Now at first, I thought, "used Bible, there may be other marks, underlines, highlighter, circles," . . . no, apparently not! I haven't found any! Verse 5 says, "The light shines in the darkness, but the darkness has not understood it." When I made this discovery, my green-light book was a finished and complete project. Once again, I'm seeing something that I cannot explain. I had a strong emotional moment . . . maybe a little more than a moment.

Shortly after my book was published, I went to a print shop to get some cards printed up – business card size with a similar image and design as the book cover. I've been looking for any opportunity to hand them out and share my experience using them. It's been interesting because some people have in turn shared their own divine experiences with me. But that's not always the case. Just the other day, I encountered a woman sitting down at the gym where I go to work out. I introduced myself and started chatting and then shortly thereafter asked if she was a Christian. She stated that she wasn't. I went on to tell her about my green-light experience. She wasn't impressed in the least and stated that she has seen lights all the time, in either mysterious or not-so-mysterious ways. I put forth a little more effort into my story, but to no avail. She remained unimpressed.

Speaking of sharing my story with others, and to be expected, I've heard comments like I should've contacted the Air Force, check the drugs I'm taking, etc. As for drugs, I don't take any. No prescribed ones either. In the last 5 years or so, I've taken maybe a total of 6 aspirin tablets. That's it. And alcohol . . . I'm a beer and wine guy, wine almost always with food. I can have beer by itself but I've got to be thirsty for it, and I'm almost never thirsty for too much beer in the winter. So, to clarify, I did not consume any, or enough alcohol to make me see strange lights, of this I am certain. God, the Almighty, came by my bedroom that night, to either say, "You're welcome," or, "I heard you." Of this, I am also certain.

CHAPTER TWO

FRIENDS, PARENTS, TEACHERS...

MY FRIEND GALE.

Now here is a true-life event experienced by a wife and a mother that should truly inspire every Christian to re-establish your faith in God and Jesus. I asked Gale to meet with me so we could discuss specific details about the loss of her husband. She agreed and we met yesterday for lunch. Gale and I got to know each other several years ago – maybe about 7 or 8 now. She was looking for some help with her tennis game and found out that I could help her with that. Had the Almighty not have used our mutual interest in tennis, we would have never met! But the Lord uses whatever He wishes to make things happen! I am so very glad that she and I are friends and she is my sister-in-Christ. Her faith in God and Jesus is amazing and so very inspiring.

I'm guessing it was about the year 2005 when her husband was late coming home from work. A major part of his duties involved driving a truck. Here in Texas, you can get a mean glare from the sun just above the horizon just before dusk. This was the best guess made since her husband did not survive the accident. Traffic was stopped ahead and he was unable to stop in time. As more time passed, finally the doorbell rang and when their middle daughter opened the door, Gale stated that there were about a dozen people standing on her porch. She knew right then that something was terribly wrong. So here now is a wife and mother of three daughters – one in high school, one in middle school, and a two-year old. Gale feels an eye-jarring slap of reality across her face. Her knees bent and her legs began to buckle as she felt the weight of "her cross" leaning heavily on her back.

But I will stop right there with the boo-hoo stuff. Today, Gale's faith and her relationship with God and Jesus is a new and victorious story, one of love and sacrifice, and her trust in the Almighty. The good fruit of this tree is a testament to her incredible faith. Her daughters are beautiful, on the outside and inside, but my specific reference is to the inside. And now the fruits of her strength are showing with her one grandson. Gale shared that her pastor and church were there to help during the worst of times, and clearly she had the wisdom to request and receive the help. Gale told me that she became a Christian and was "saved" in her twenties.

Gale's cross now leans up against a wall, on its own. Occasionally, it may slip and start to fall, but with a quick "Help me, Lord" it's back up against the wall. Her legs and her back are now as strong as they will ever be, strengthened with unshakable faith in the Almighty. She is a living, laughing, tennis-racquet-swinging, walking proof of God's work -- God's good work with humanity. God's great work! God has provided me with a one-time Light experience to see and marvel about, and He has put in my hands a Bible "marked" to confirm His Light, and no less, a friend who's living faith in God serves to me as an earthly inspiration as well.

A SURPRISE FOR THE KIDDOS.

Here's something that I think most parents can appreciate. You have a surprise planned for the kiddos that of course they don't know about. Let's say you and your spouse have it scheduled for a Saturday. Now the kids, thinking about their Saturday, may have plans of their own. So, when you inform them that you've got other ideas in mind and their intended plans won't be happening, they are bummed, and of course, are now curious as to what's going on. Since it's a surprise, you can't tell them and you remain evasive to their questions, and you tell them to just "trust you." You also tell them that they'll be happy with your surprise. Now, I'm going somewhere specific with this so the actual surprise or event really doesn't matter. It could be an outing at a theme park, a pool party with friends and family, whatever, but as their parents you know what it is they are going to enjoy, which as loving parents is why you planned it in the first place. It will warm your heart watching your kids smile and laugh as they enjoy the surprise activity.

Do you know what Heaven is? I don't. We have to "trust" God that as our Father, we are going to love it. We are His kiddos. We know all too well what our Saturdays are like. In this example, I have not yet brought out the "brat" kiddo. The one who doesn't care about the surprise, the one who had their Saturday planned and wants to see it through. The one who doesn't trust in your decision and your planned event. As parents, we are saddened by what we're hearing and seeing, and now, knowing that our kiddos don't trust us as parents. They don't realize that there is *no one* anywhere on this Earth that loves them more than us!

But as parents we understand that they are young and immature. If we love them and exercise patience with them, hoping that one day they too will understand love and trust, then we can fully realize this concept of child, trust, and parent. If we consider how easy it is for a parent to love a child, the doubts and distractions for children, and the time and experiences for their trust and faith to develop, then maybe we can better understand that our parent is God, we are His children, and hopefully at some point in our lives we too will trust. The sooner the better, but later works, too. Remember the parable Jesus shared of the Vineyard Owner: that even those hired at the latter part of the day received the same wages as those he hired first.

I don't know what to expect when I enter the Kingdom of God, and I will enter it, because Jesus paid my debt, and He paid yours, too! John 3:16 says it all. I trust that there is where I will want to be and nowhere else!

A THANK YOU LETTER.

Here's some much needed acknowledgement for "loving parents." First, I want to thank parents who, despite really wanting to end their marriage, have thought first and more of their kids and how divorce would affect their development. It may never be known how your sacrifice saved this world from a seriously troubled child.

Next, and no less important, are the divorced parents who remain civil and friendly and patient and considerate and co-operative with the other parent, so that their children don't have to be put in the middle of a whole bunch of crap. Thank you, divorced mom! Thank you, divorced dad! Marriage is becoming less and less important with today's society and it shows, especially with the steady number of divorces. I'm not trying to blame anyone for divorcing, as I'm twice guilty of it myself. I've heard over the years -- just a few times, though, about parents who had the foresight to consider how their actions in the present with the other parent impacts a child in a major way. Thank you again for what you're doing, and not doing! May God bless you, and I mean that sincerely! Some parents fail to realize that the actions they're taking are being witnessed, and most importantly, will be remembered and may never be forgotten. The parents are forgetting that their child is "half", or part, of that other parent, and that child still loves that parent. They didn't ask to be born nor did they ask for the divorce. And now the kids have become instruments of revenge and they want their kids to hate the other parent just like they do!

If you truly love your children, then don't do this to them anymore! These negative actions will have the biggest impact on children, not adults. And the impacts can and probably will be life-long. Stop it! Most of us are familiar with some daytime TV shows concerning paternity tests. Who or why someone decided that these make worthy entertainment, I don't know! To drive a car one needs a license, and in some areas permits are required to hold a yard sale or even to sell lemonade, yet to have a child . . . nada, nothing! I don't have specific answers here, but I do have questions. Why is this so? And another question on top. Why is no one, that I know of, asking questions either? Or better yet, offering suggestions or solutions?!

I recall several years ago when my youngest son was having typical teenage issues, and I did some research. I discovered that teenagers, especially boys, were in the development phase of their "pre-frontal cortex." Complete development of the cortex may not occur until the early to mid-20s. This was and is *science*. I didn't make this stuff up. Isn't it still science?

To my understanding, the pre-frontal cortex plays a major role in logical or better decision-making. These days, we're hearing a lot about "transgender" issues. Boys thinking they're girls and vice-versa. I've even heard that in some states, parents can be charged with a crime for interfering with their kids' transgender desires. What I haven't heard at all is the pre-frontal cortex argument against any such case of transgender issues or subsequent medical procedures.

Why anyone would allow a child to make a drastic decision concerning life-altering surgeries is beyond my understanding!

TEACHER TIME.

We can all recall a time when a teacher stated, "I can see that he or she is really trying." Whether it was said for us or our kids, we realize that the teacher recognizes the effort that the student has been putting forth. And sometimes, that may be the best the student can do. And by this teacher statement, we can assume that the teacher is satisfied with the student's attempts at the task or subject.

In the Bible it is written that God searches our hearts. If God went solely by our works and deeds, there would be no reason to search our hearts. Our actions would define us. But God being the Ultimate Teacher with His infinite wisdom extends His patience to His students who may never "completely get it," but are trying and know that they must always keep trying.

A reminder here: Very few of us are A+ students with God, but that's okay. God is perfect, we're not, and He knows this. Like that teacher, He wants to see that we're trying. Plus, He knows our hearts.

Grab one of your hands, now put it on your chest, left side. Feel your heartbeat? Yes, I hope so! What is the power-source for that beating? D-size batteries? Solar panels? 'Tis not! It is the Almighty! So, if the Lord gave you another day to live, there's a reason: to do something or to learn something, or both. So go ahead… suggestions: forgive someone, read a Christian book, attend a church service… What are you waiting for?

DEAR FRIEND, I'M SORRY.

I'm sorry you don't or can't see what I see! I'm sorry you can't hear what I hear. And I'm really sorry you don't know what I know! You don't know that our God is all around, that despite all the craziness of today's world, He is totally in control. I'm sorry that your view is out of focus, and there is so much to see that is right in front of your eyes, and yet you fail to see it. The beauty of a flower, the twinkle in the eyes of a child, the warmth of a smile in your mother or father or brother or friend. Why are there so many colors and varieties of flowers and scents? Why do we have senses in our noses to notice these scents? Why?! Because our God made us that way! Why did He do this? I'll tell you why! To see just ONE thing He can do with a flower. Just ONE thing, among the billions or trillions of other things He has made for us to notice and appreciate. Why can we smile? Why can we laugh? I'm sorry you can't smile. I'm sorry you haven't laughed today or yesterday, or last week! I'm sorry your attitude doesn't include reasons to find happiness despite all you have been blessed with! I'm sorry you can't take a look around and see God everywhere! Any birds around you singing? And dogs around wagging their tails? Any wonder around or something to marvel at? If not, I'm sorry. I'm sorry you're stuck on your couch or staring at your phone. I'm sorry simplicity confounds you. I'm sorry truth frustrates you. I'm sorry you have a sibling that you haven't spoken to in years because of something that happened decades ago, and you can't let it go. I'm sorry. I'm sorry that you believe that the only thing that you have in this world to turn to is booze or pot or some other drug. I'm sorry, friend. I really am.

LET'S SAY YOU WANT A DOG --

a puppy to start with. You find one. You pay the cost, whatever that is, get shots, etc. You buy the premium food for it, toys, a fancy doggie bed. You're all in with this pooch. As the puppy grows it does typical puppy stuff like peeing here and there, chewing up shoes, clothes, your new wallet, so on and so on. Over the years you've spent now with the pooch, you've given it a lot of your time and affection. However, poochie hasn't reciprocated much at all. It doesn't greet you when you get home. Basically, it just doesn't act like it should, or how you would expect it to act after giving this creature so much. You would probably ask yourself, "Why did I even get this ungrateful dog?!" And you might even think about getting rid of it. Why wouldn't you? It isn't doing anything good.

A reasonable and natural reaction here is to give up on this dog, right? That's what my reaction would be. Let's call this dog Spot.

Different dog -- Rover. Rover is the exact opposite of Spot. Rover can't wait for you to come home, loves licking your face, loves to cuddle with you, and to protect you, etc. Simple question and simple answer: Which dog would you prefer to have, own, and claim? An attitude of gratitude reveals so much! There are several perspectives that one can view this Spot/Rover example.

ARE YOU A PARENT? THE REASON

I ask is because I believe a parent can appreciate a little more deeply what I'm about to write. Let's imagine, you, an adult: man or woman, aunt or uncle, or a trusted friend who is watching, baby-sitting, keeping an eye on, or entertaining a child at your residence. You're the adult in charge. Suddenly you've become aware of a possible danger to the child. Your first thought is to protect the child, right? Hypothetical situation here, so the exact issue doesn't matter – a stranger trying to break in, a snake slithering through a window, whatever. You, caring for this child, will do whatever you need to, to keep the child safe. Okay, you get it -- you, your home, you're in charge and you're not going to let anything happen to this child, or any other child on your watch. I illustrate this scenario because of what I witness at church every time I attend. That is, those who do not want to shake hands when it's time to extend a sign of peace. While in God's house, they're scared?!

I realize, of course, that this is my opinion on the matter, but the entire book is pretty much my opinion. Anyway, I believe that while I'm in one of God's houses, celebrating Him and His Son, that I am protected by God Himself. Why would God allow some funky cooties to harm me while in His house, honoring Him? He wouldn't! That's my belief. And I think everybody in a church, truly believing and celebrating God's Love (Jesus) should trust in that protection, as well. Consider my prefaced example. God would allow this – catching cooties – while in His home, and honoring Him? Not my God!

So if we, mere mortals, would do all to protect a child from harm, wouldn't God Almighty protect us in His house, while honoring Him and His Son? Why yes, He would and does! So, smile and shake them hands, and save the peace signs for folks two pews over!

CHAPTER THREE

QUESTIONS, ADAM
AND EVE ...

AS I WROTE IN MY PREVIOUS book, I have a lot of questions concerning what's written in the Bible, and what's not written. Now, as we know, God put Adam in a deep sleep to remove his rib, but could God have made an addition? It is written that Adam did not find any of the other creatures that God made suitable for him. Thus, God made Eve. Now if God made Adam first and without a woman in mind, why would Adam need testicles? Adam could have a penis, of course, for peeing, but at that point why would testicles be needed?

We know that testicles are needed to produce testosterone and sperm. Testosterone for an erection and sperm for conception. If Adam was originally created without testicles, which again I point out, if no Eve, why are they needed? Then the Lord must have added them to Adam sometime after he was originally created. I would guess, since he was already "under" getting a rib out, go ahead and do it then?! Unless, did the Lord know about Eve beforehand, and maybe wanted Adam to ask for her, or, was Adam's rib "needed" to create Eve? There are foods and herbs that can aid and increase the production of testosterone. Could the "tree of life", as written about in the Book of Genesis, have possibly produced a fruit that would greatly increase the production of testosterone? The Lord had the tree of life guarded by cherubim with a flaming sword to prevent man from living forever, assuming they would continue to eat from this tree.

At this point, Adam and Eve had already failed their first test and broke the Lord's only commandment, but yet, the Lord did not want them to continue eating from the tree.

Since Adam and Eve can now discern between good and evil, what evil was there to notice? No other people around. No killing, yet. No robbing, adultery, etc. My guess comes down to sex or lust, which, if one consumes something that produces aphrodisiac results, sexual acts would be expected.

If you've watched any TV in the last few years, you couldn't miss commercials about "testosterone-boosting" products for the older guy. And, of course, wink-wink, the woman will benefit too! Why does our testosterone gradually dwindle with age? Is this why we are supposed to become wiser the older we get? Less hormones and less aggression? Less re-acting and more thinking? We're now using our brains more? Maybe this dwindling shouldn't be happening? Maybe our modern-day diets are to blame? Our environmental issues like pollution in the air and water, or mental stressors are contributing factors?

Now Adam and Eve created the first humans by natural conception and birth. From what the Bible tells us, they had two sons, Cain and Abel. In line with my "testosterone" questions, here we already have a murderer. Too much testosterone? We know that "fratricide" is a common occurrence, but, not that common. Most people murdered are not killed by a sibling.

We know from several sources, including the Bible, that a great flood occurred on Earth some time ago. God regretted creating Man and decided to notify one man – Noah – and his family. God found favor with Noah as he was a righteous man. The rest of mankind was filled with violence, and a new breed of man would arise from the seed of Noah. God instructed Noah about how to build an ark, and to gather animals of each species, male and female. Mankind in the time of Noah was a violent breed. For violence, aggression is needed. Testosterone is needed for aggression. So, we know about the flood, Noah, and the Ark.

Next, Sodom and Gomorrah. Cities filled with, well, sodomy and more violence. A few things to consider before I move forward, and to put into context. We're talking about events that happened thousands of years ago. It's too easy to imagine this now and to not consider life and typical everyday activities for people back then. To eat, one must grow, bake, hunt, kill, prepare, and cook your food. There are no refrigerators, appliances, etc. There is no plumbing. I'm trying to figure out how, with so much to do, how can anyone have energy for sex? Heck, even going back just about a hundred and fifty years ago, life wasn't so easy then, either. The Bible doesn't explain much about everyday activities, but from what we can gather, cities did function in some typical ways as today: taxes were collected; someone ruled or was in charge of running the city along with subordinates; there was a defending army; a water source was needed; goods and services were produced. All of this, though, required work, hard work. No comfy couch to nap in, no springy mattress to get in eight hours of restful sleep. There were no arch supports to put in your shoes to help your tired feet. There were no shoes! So, apparently, testosterone was not in short supply. I guess another point to consider would be "association." When men hang around men, their traits and characteristics rub off on each other. So, if not-so-tough guys hang a lot with tough guys, Won't the not-so-tough guys try to emulate the tough guys? Will not the dominant members of the species dominate the weaker? What does the dominant man have a lot of? Testosterone?! Will we need testosterone in Heaven? No! What for? What would a world be like without testosterone? What exactly is testosterone?

Let's imagine a drawing of a man, like a centuries-old one by DaVinci or Michelangelo or one of those Renaissance artists: that naked guy with his arms stretched out. What is at his center? His crotch (and testes), of course. For decades, that too was my center, and I have no doubt, for billions, or greater, of other men as well. Center, the bullseye of this world. Now a perspective change, same guy. How did God design us? Top spot: the head (and brain). Where we think, learn, realize. And just below the head is our heart, where after thinking, learning, or realizing, or all of them, we feel. A link exists between the two where both are used to make critically important decisions. Decisions that will affect our souls and where we will end up throughout eternity!

The human brain: what a marvelous piece of work by our God! There truly aren't enough words to describe such, and that originally started out as a part of a sperm cell and an egg!

The human heart (my favorite). You can't tell me that its power source isn't the breath of God! That's all I can believe, what else is there?! To me, our hearts represent our souls. Yet our souls do not belong to us. God made them, and he will decide after careful examination what to do with them! Is your heart good? God is good. Is it forgiving? God is forgiving. Is it loving? God is loving! Well . . .?

And at the bottom, the crotch. Extremely important, wouldn't you say?! We wouldn't be here if our parents didn't use it! Isn't it awesome that God gave us the power to create little versions of ourselves?!?

So, with this better perspective, our brains are first with an all-important and integral link with our hearts. Crotch stuff at the bottom and not at the center of one's life. Testosterone clearly has a role to play in our lives but it shouldn't be at the top.

A few more questions:

In which language did the Lord speak to Adam and Eve? Since they were created and not raised from a child's age, their brains were already fully formed, yes? What age were they? We know the learning of language is a slow process and is completed in stages for children. However, Adam and Eve were not children when created so the Lord created them with the ability to speak and understand a language. So, I ask what language was that?

And did the other creatures have the ability to speak? Eve didn't seem surprised that a serpent could talk!?

I've thought long and hard about my questions, thoughts, and pretty much this entire chapter and whether it should be left in the book. As one can see, I decided to leave it in. I'm thinking that when I do get to Heaven, I'll just be tickled to be there, and I will no longer care about questions or answers.

CHAPTER FOUR

EVIL: YOU KNOW WHO

SATAN EXISTS: YES OR NO?

A topic most prefer to avoid. Easy to understand why, but how wise is it to do so? The Bible provides us with numerous occasions and referrals to Satan, including evil and unclean spirits. There are many professionals and the like who have discounted possessions written in the Bible as mental or physical illnesses. Yes or no: Does the Bible have it wrong? In the Book of Luke, Jesus refers to Satan and his kingdom. We also know that Jesus was tempted by Satan in the desert.

Well? Would now be a good time to finally decide? Does he indeed exist? If so, where is he right now? Who is he tempting? If Satan made an attempt with Jesus Himself, why wouldn't he try with others in power? Is Satan smart enough to utilize the business plan of "working smarter, not harder"? Why not hit the head of a large corporation or organization, with their massive followers, members, employees, along with social media and marketing influencers? He is the "father of lies," right? Let's say he just woke up from a hundred-year nap right now, and he turned on the TV. What would his reaction be? Would he sigh or smile, or maybe get up and start laughing and dancing in delight?

Now if one denies the existence of something, yet it really does exist, then its existence will not be addressed, and its existence will remain unchallenged.

Let's face it, almost everybody I know NEVER speaks of Satan! People don't want to talk about or even acknowledge that he does exist. I'm guessing some people think that if they do, others will think them in need of psychological help, or a religious fanatic. But the fact remains, if one truly believes in God and Jesus, and all that's in the Bible, then Satan is as real as this book you are holding. So again, I ask, where is he right now?

Who is he tempting? The Bible describes him as wise and cunning. He clearly understands man as he's been around long enough. What about his buddies? In my first book, I describe and detail some dark events that I witnessed and experienced. What about my friend Gale and her setback? I'm certain evil was cruising her neighborhood when it heard the cries and saw the commotion at her home. "Ooh, easy pickings here. This lady will be boozing or hooked on painkillers, and her 3 daughters will be smoking and toking before you know it!" NOT! NOPE! Ain't happening with this family! Don't you remember, Evil Spirit? Passing by on those Sunday mornings, as you were headed to the party house down the block, the meth, weed, and crack all-night Saturday night party? Now those partiers were real easy pickings! No, but here's a challenge, because you do remember now. On those Sunday mornings, this family was always walking down the driveway, with baby in one hand and a Bible in the other! Heading to church. Oh well, there are others, so many others! So many that don't even believe that you exist. So many that don't believe in anything! No challenge, though. How easy they must be! But Satan has such an easy goal: ignore God. That's it!

Satan doesn't need you to be his biggest fan! You don't need to go and buy dark candles or dark robes or start a club! Just . . . ignore God. Satan is completely satisfied with just that.

This needs repeating! If all you do is "ignore God," Satan is satisfied with that!

So, something got me thinking during the whole Covid craze. The supply chain issues we were dealing with, specifically the computer chip issue where the production of new cars was affected, etc. It was common to see during a TV news report: chip production workers all dressed up in their sterile, white suits with the masks, goggles, booties, etc. So, in order to work in this environment, one must be as clean and germ-free and dust-free as possible. Now if you or I were to attempt to walk right into one of these facilities, just as we would normally, we would not be allowed. Why not? We showered this morning, and put on clean clothes. Well, we know why: Because even though we brushed our teeth, shampooed our hair, put on deodorant and all that, we're just not "clean enough!" Entering into one of these facilities just as we are could contaminate whatever it is that needs to be super-clean and spotless. Otherwise, the sterile integrity of the facility would be compromised. Which brings me to the word Jesus uses often to describe man. And that word is "evil."

Clarifying "evil"

In the Bible we find Jesus referring to man several times as "evil." Now I think it a natural reaction for most people to consider this term as undeserved or unfitting. I know that I felt this initially. However, we must consider language translations here. I'm assuming that much of the Bible was written in several languages: Aramaic, Hebrew, Greek, and maybe some others. I am not a Bible scholar by any stretch of the imagination, but I do know these languages are safe to point out. Another possible point to consider about the term "evil" that Jesus uses is context. Another synonym used in the Bible for evil is "unclean." Many times, it can be found when describing "spirits" and the possessions of people. Of course, Jesus was quite accurate to say that indeed there are "evil" people here on the Earth, but I think the point He was trying to make was that even a little bit of evil won't make it through the entrance of Heaven. As human babies, and as children and teenagers, almost always our entire focus is on me/us. Some very old people die with that same unchanged focus! Human nature is "I." I want! I need! I'm hungry! I'm in the mood for this . . . or that! Humans are self-ish. To be clear, I am selfish! As we grow and age and become older and wiser, we're given countless opportunities to "learn" and become less selfish, and to learn to love more. We can come to learn that things – material things – are just things. We can learn that there is so much more to life.

Well, what can we learn as we live? Much! Maybe the first thing we should consider is that life is for learning. Not textbooks, schools, and higher education. I mean, not just that type of learning. I mean human-experience learning. Things that have no degree or certification. Things that only your soul can know and feel. Things that align with the words and actions of God and Jesus. Things that make sense to your heart. Things that bring you peace. These are the types of learning experiences I'm referring to. Ideally, thinking less of "Me" and more of "He" would be best. Since the beginning man has wondered about death and feared it. If we come to trust the sacrifice Jesus made on the cross, then we can learn and trust that death is merely a step into God's Kingdom.

Again, death is something we don't think about – not usually. But if there's one thing that I can say most assuredly is that one day I will die, and you will, too. My days are numbered and so are yours, and tomorrow morning when we awake, there will be one less day on the total count. And there is nothing, not one worldly thing that you now own that you can take with you on that last day. Not your adorable pet, your favorite child, not even a single penny of your bulging bank account! The only thing you have when you die is your soul! Now, right now, is a great time to take stock of your soul. Checked it lately? You have one! It may be deep in your heart, or maybe close to the surface. What's it filled with? Love? Hate? Pity? Resentment? I'm guessing that like most people, it's a jumble of stuff. But now's a good time to sort that all out!

So, what does God owe us? Nothing! We've been provided with an earthly life. We've been blessed with health, a career or job, a home, children. What are you lacking? Probably not much! When your life here on Earth ends, what do you want? What do you expect? We don't remember anything before we were born. There was "nothing" before we were born, individually speaking. Do you want nothing again? Clearly, almost all of us love something here on Earth. For most of us, there is much we love! If you knew your life would end tomorrow, how would you feel, and what would you do? Only if your life was horribly bad would your reaction be, "Okay, no problem." For some reason, though, thinking about our death is something we just don't do. Each and every one of us will experience it. One day it will come, that is for certain. Is "nothing" okay for you on that day?

Do you like majestic mountain tops, awesome sunsets, deep blue skies with big, white, puffy clouds? I could go on and on. What to expect in Heaven?! Well, if God created all this beautiful stuff here on Earth, I could only expect even better in Heaven! Plus, no more hate, no more evil, no more brutality, no more pain, no more tears! And yet, the way and answer is so simple . . . Jesus! We all have questions! I have quite a lot! But I have more faith than questions, because I know that my faith in Jesus is most important. Open your heart.

CHAPTER FIVE

MOVIES, HISTORY, THE WORLD

I CAME UP WITH AN IDEA

because of my younger son. Apparently, there was much about history – U.S. and the world -- that he was unaware of. I also realized this would be helpful to a lot of people, young and old. I didn't realize what he was being taught and what he wasn't being taught, especially about our country's history. The history of our country really can't be separated from the world's. Everything about the founding of our country was due to or inspired from previous historical events. My great idea was to have him watch movies that dealt with important historical events. There are a lot of good movies available to watch and learn from. There are those based on historical events, and people who don't know much about world and U.S. history can learn from them, and more importantly, figure out that our country is quite exceptional.

All of the movies deal with war and the conquering of other countries by methods of war and brutality. War and brutality are synonymous. Kings, queens, and dictators live comfortably while they send out their generals and armies to do the dirty work and to satisfy their greed and egos. (*Glory* excluded.) While we have to stretch our imaginations to appreciate these movies in full, our founding fathers wouldn't have had to. The brutality of war and battle, the greed of kings and rulers were their reality. This is all they knew. They did have to stretch their imaginations to envision a country unlike any other. They had to fight and make tremendous sacrifices all while knowing that by losing the American Revolution they would lose all they had achieved, as well as their lives.

It's difficult to go back two thousand years to view world history accurately. We can't even go back two hundred years to view our own country's history from a proper and complete perspective. So many people today are oblivious and ignorant about U.S. history before their own existence. And most unfortunately, so many of these are just fine with remaining that way. One requires imagination to go back in time and consider all the aspects of our past history, but with smartphones, computers, and A.I., who needs imagination?

Throughout human history, ALL countries and their rulers have attacked, invaded, killed, burned, raped, and pillaged other lands and territories. We tend to easily forget, because it's been a while since bigger conflicts like World War II, the Korean War, and the Vietnam War. But we get frequent reminders. Like now, as I write this, Hamas just attacked Israel and brutally murdered innocent civilians. It's one thing to attack an armed, uniformed soldier, but something else entirely to kill those in the process of living their normal lives. So even now, at the end of this year 2023, brutality continues.

So, watch and learn! And then go read and learn some more! The honorable men who carefully constructed the documents that founded our great country risked everything in doing so. Our freedom was not "free"! Signing their names on those documents meant those same names were on the British Traitor List. And on the East Coast of this country in the late 1770s, that is a list you did NOT want to be on! But for freedom, equality, and an end to brutality, these men imagined something greater – a country that recognized and revered God.

And speaking of wars and religion and God, I've encountered a lot of people in my life who blamed religion/God for the wars in history. However, that is mostly Man's doing, and it certainly was not the teachings of Christ! It was Jesus himself stating that those who draw/take the sword shall die by it. Jesus instructed his followers to "shake the dust" from their feet/sandals of those who didn't want to accept His word. That's it! "Religion" was often used as a means or excuse to invade, take over, or kill.

Now, if I could only use one word to describe the history of mankind it would be "brutality." A strong, and obvious, theme in most of these films is just that. Humans have been killing and murdering each other for a long time. On every continent and in every nation. Why? Maybe not so difficult to figure out, but it will be if examined through 21st century eyes. Let's go back when there were no nations, only groups of people – or tribes. Your group against mine, or your tribe against mine. If one tribe starts getting stronger with more procreation, more livestock, more land, bigger and more accurate weapons, then what? A tribe may feel vulnerable, or a tribe may feel stronger than those nearby. These are times when everything must be worked for – from the water supply to the food eaten, to the clothes on your back and the roof over your head. If you're hungry you must pick it, grow it, or kill it and prepare it for cooking. If you're thirsty you find a stream or river, or dig a well.

HERE ARE MY CHOICES OF MOVIES

for learning: *Gladiator* (2000); *Braveheart* (1995); *The Last of the Mohicans* (1992); *The Patriot* (2000); *The Bounty (Mutiny on the Bounty)* (1984); and *Glory* (1989). Sit, watch, be entertained, and LEARN, all on your comfy couch. What a simple concept: No textbooks, no need to study. Pop some popcorn or grab some chips and relax.

GLADIATOR

A well-acted, entertaining movie set in the year 180 AD. A century and a half after Christ walked the Earth. The superior and all-powerful Roman Army has but one final battle left to conquer all enemies. The opening scene shows the Romans preparing to engage the enemy with all the best available weapons there were at the time. In full command and control is Maximus the General, strategizing the attack. It's an easy victory, at least in the movie. (Reality may have been a different story.) Nonetheless, it's a Roman victory. A frontal attack prepped with huge fireballs, massive arrows – all launched with the latest military technology (for the 2nd century).

No doubt, the Germanian barbarians – at least a few – peed in their pants watching six-foot arrows stake a fellow comrade to the ground or a tree. An unexpected attack from the rear seals the outcome, as the Germanian forces are divided, and thus conquered. Divide and conquer – a simple strategy – highly effective and still in use today.

Okay, the military battles are over. Now, a new set of struggles to address: shall the government of Rome be ruled by a dictating Caesar or be a Senate-involved Republic? Caesar's daughter, Lucilla, has admirable qualities to rule: she's patient, diplomatic, and wise. However, she's a woman. Not a problem in this day and age, but not happening in the 2nd century. Caesar's son, Commodus, lacks all the qualities to make a just, wise, and honorable leader. So, Caesar chooses Maximus, his General, to succeed him. Problems, though: Maximus doesn't want the job, which is a big reason why Caesar wants him to have it. And, Commodus does! Commodus is left with no choice but to kill his father and to kill Maximus and his family so that he can rule Rome.

BRAVEHEART

Braveheart is a movie about the legendary William Wallace of Scotland. As with all big release movies, I expect, directors, producers, etc., exercised creative license in the making of. I also expect the main theme of the movie is true to historical events, which for my purposes, is all that matters. England's king wants to and does rule Scotland. The king is cunning, ruthless, and will stop at nothing to maintain power. Wallace, who is basically just a peasant, is forced to take up arms and rebel against the king. There's a love story intertwined in the film and I do not know about the historical accuracy concerning that.

Wallace fights for the independence of Scotland, and of course, realizes that if this is not achieved, his death will be. I think it likely that our founding fathers probably knew of Wallace and the English/Scottish battles. Clearly, Wallace had guts, which were removed at his execution. He must have been a man with strong leadership qualities to rally peasants with stones and sticks to challenge the seasoned soldiers and armies of England.

Before Wallace can see Scotland finally win its freedom from England, he is captured and executed without mercy by the king. His bravery and unwillingness to accept nothing less than complete freedom for his country inspires those who follow to continue the fight until victory is achieved.

THE LAST OF THE MOHICANS

Here's a great flick. It's based in Colonial America around the 1750s. The British and the French, along with Native American allies, are engaging in vicious combat over forts and territory. No mention of future American military leaders like George Washington. America's battle with the British is still a couple of decades to come. There's a love story well-entangled in the movie. It adds another dimension to the historical fact that even love and romance were difficult to engage in around an 18th century war.

Despite the love story, there's plenty of in-your-face violence that was a part of real history. Now this film was originally a book written in the early 19th century. I've never read it and I don't know if it had the love story in it. Unimportant though, as this book – my book – attempts to illustrate the historical aspects of this land and event.

THE BOUNTY (MUTINY ON THE BOUNTY)

This is a great film. The versions I've seen even going back to Clark Gable's or to the latest – Mel Gibson's – are very well-acted. This film shows the cold reality of military service under the queen and British rule. "Do" as ordered, or death or imprisonment. Nothing or little is yours. All is for England. Whether a sailor on this ship or a soldier fighting the Scots of William Wallace, your life means little. On the chessboard of life, you are a mere pawn. One must use their imagination to realize that these same British ships were stationed on the U.S. East Coast – as in Boston Harbor – during the American Revolution, and were also being used as prisons to hold American Army soldiers or anyone helping the American side or cause.

Can anyone even begin to imagine imprisonment on an 18th century military ship? A starvation diet, rats, no sunlight or fresh air, sleep on the floor, and probably a wet or damp floor. And if that isn't torture enough, some real torture. I think most people can't even begin to imagine such! Yet these were realities for all those who helped in the founding of OUR country. Many of us know the names of the signers of our constitution, but all of us don't know most of those who sacrificed everything to start a new country. We will never know the thousands of names of those who paid the ultimate sacrifice for the founding of this country! Safe to say that now, in these times, there are millions of school-age students and even adults who aren't even aware of the countless unsung heroes who helped establish this great country.

THE PATRIOT

The Patriot stars Mel Gibson and Heath Ledger. This movie is about the American Revolution against England and the fight for our independence. I'm going to skim over this one because this film contains a lot of personal details with the main character's life and family, of which I'm assuming is fiction. Of course, these details revolve around the war, which is not fiction. There is much to watch and the film facilitates the imagination to consider the hardships, the sacrifices, and the brutality of war and life in the 1700s.

GLORY

Glory is another great film with talented actors like Denzel Washington, Matthew Broderick, and Morgan Freeman. This movie deals with our Civil War and the first fighting regiment of black Union soldiers. A good part of the movie covers the preliminaries of military training and racial obstacles of the time period. I'm guessing some of the interpersonal dialogue between some characters may have been fiction. Some of the characters may be fictional, too, but Broderick's character seems to be factual. The story may have actually come from the commander's own personal diary. The events of this regiment seem to be fact, as well. One element missing from this film is the burying of dead soldiers. Another is the medical treatment for battle-injured soldiers, as amputating limbs was common. There was no anesthesia, as surgery was a handful of men to hold you down, maybe a shot of whiskey, a bullet to bite on, oh, and a hacksaw!

No doubt, everyone present probably suffered from PTSD! If you've ever heard the saying, "bite the bullet," that's its origin. Our Civil War had the most American casualties of any war in our history. When you watch this film, add these aspects to it to help you understand our history. We got to add our own American flavor of brutality to the world's.

SO, WHERE AM I GOING WITH these historical films? Over the last few years, we've been hearing about how our United States is and has been an awful country – full of racists, exploiters, etc. However, when the U.S. is compared in context with all countries historically since the beginning of recorded history, one can only come to the conclusion that our country has done the most for equality, freedom, prosperity, religion, etc. And all at a very great cost! It's way too easy to not think about or even know what sacrifices were made by thousands upon thousands of unsung heroes. The sixteen-year-old boys that had no choice but to fight the British armies. The seventeen-year-olds caught up in unwanted civil war. The eighteen-year-old young men who climbed into Air Force bombers or served below in Navy ships. I'll bet countless died before ever even getting to kiss a young lady!

You don't know the sacrifices made for this country, and for you and me! And if you don't know, then you may not care, and if you don't care then you won't honor. But worse yet, we have countless that want to and prefer to dishonor this country. All . . . out of ignorance!

These films provide a glimpse of nation relations, nation-building and expansion, and war, killing, and brutality. Throughout history, my guess is that ninety-nine percent of humanity were expendable pawns. Only those who ruled had value and did all they could to remain in power.

Conclusion: You will have quite a difficult task to find a land, a tribe, a nation throughout our world's history that did not oppress, exploit, pillage, destroy, sack, brutalize another group of people or nation in order to preserve or expand their own. In comparison to other nations of the world, our country is relatively new. Changes and progress take time, especially in older times. Our Founding Fathers recognized where changes were needed. Reality reminds us that change does not come easy, and not without sacrifice – as millions of those who came before us paid the ultimate price.

HERE ARE SOME MORE MOV-IES I HAVE WATCHED AND RECOMMEND:

Jesus Christ Superstar (1973)
I listened to the soundtrack/album as a kid growing up. I like the creative ideas the writers and directors brought into the film. I think it's a great movie.

Saving Private Ryan (1998)
A film centered around World War II's D-Day Invasion. Lots of blood-and-guts reality in this movie, so you can keep your imagination cap off for this one. If you can't appreciate an American soldier with this one, there's something wrong with you!

The Passion of the Christ (2004)
If you don't appreciate what Jesus did for us, then definitely watch this movie! Also, as Catholics, we usually have a cruci-fix with Jesus in church, and Jesus appears pretty clean and barely injured up there. This film will remind us how far from reality our crucifixes are!

Defiance (2008)
A moving film based on true events during World War II in Europe.

CONCLUSION

I didn't write a conclusion for the first book. Instead I ended it with "Save the Planet" tips. So, know this: God is real, and the "real deal"! In this realm and the next, there is nothing and no other that can and will love your soul, as He created it and you! If you can't or don't see God in this realm, then talk to Him (pray). Praying to God is talking to Him. Ask Him to help you see, and keep asking until you do. He will not fail you!

The world is crazy, right? Maybe your life, too? What can YOU do to help, right now? PRAY! That is right! PRAY! And don't forget to give "Thanks!" Giving thanks to God is praying too. I already know that you have much to be thankful for. Allow me to make another suggestion: Learn to make the Sign of the Cross. All Catholics are familiar with this, but it's certainly not limited to us. When done and said with sincerity, it's a prayer. With two or three fingertips, touch your forehead and say, "In the name of the Father," then touch the middle of your chest area and say, "and the Son," and then your left and then right shoulders and say, "and the Holy Spirit." By doing this, you acknowledge ALL of God and most importantly, the sacrifice Jesus made to defeat "death"!

So...pray, give thanks, and be at peace knowing "death" is just a step towards Heaven. And, if you think this book can help someone who ain't thinkin' right, pass it on! =)

to shine on those living in darkness
and in the shadow of death,
to guide our feet into the path of peace.

—LUKE 1:79